How To
Have A Dynamic
Church Prayer
Ministry

How To
Have A Dynamic
Church Prayer
Ministry

Jill Griffith

WAGNER
INSTITUTE
PUBLICATIONS

How to Have a Dynamic Church Prayer Ministry
Copyright © 1999
by Jill Griffith
ISBN 0-9667481-9-0

Published by
Wagner Institute for Practical Ministry
P.O. Box 62958
Colorado Springs, CO 80962-2958

Rights for publishing this book in other languages are contracted by Gospel Literature International (GLINT). GLINT also provides technical help for the adaptation, translation, and publishing of Bible study resources and books in scores of languages worldwide. For further information, contact GLINT, P.O. Box 4060, Ontario, CA 91761-1003, USA, Email: glintint@aol.com, or the publisher.

TABLE OF CONTENTS

INTRODUCTION

Prayer is an exciting adventure! It is the seed from which miracles sprout. And no where is prayer more vibrant than in a corporate setting where our combined faith moves the heart of God on behalf of those for whom we intercede. Each and every church has a unique opportunity to foster prayer that makes a real difference both inside and outside the church walls. It is toward seeing that kind of prayer established in local churches that this manual has been written.

What is prayer? Prayer is simply talking to God. What is intercession? Intercession is simply talking to God on someone else's behalf. How can the local church raise up an army of intercessors to pray and intercede effectively? It is both simple and exciting. Statistics show that individuals commit to those things in which they have an interest and enjoy doing. The same is true of prayer. If people are interested and find it enjoyable, they will pray. Therefore, provide a smorgasbord of prayer opportunities from which people can choose.

This training manual offers a variety of prayer ministry opportunities designed to appeal to a broad church audience. By providing such opportunities, churches allow people to pray for the areas God has put on their hearts. For example, some will want to pray for a police officer by joining the "Shield a Badge With Prayer" ministry. Women and teenage girls may have a heart to pray for children in the "Cradle a Child With Prayer" ministry. Men, on the other hand, may have more of a desire to pray for those in authority in the "Adopt a Leader" prayer ministry. Whole Sunday school classes or home groups may want to adopt a grandparent through the "PrayCare for the Elderly" ministry.

This step-by-step manual will walk you through how to start, mobilize, train and launch a local church prayer ministry with this kind of variety, in addition to implementing the watch of the Lord, which has the potential of involving an entire church in prayer.

God is creative and cannot be limited. Neither should we limit ourselves on how we communicate with Him. I pray and believe that you and your local church will receive many more ideas for a prayer ministry than what I have presented here. Spread the word—there is power in our prayers! The Bible tells us in James 5:16 that the effectual fervent prayers of the righteous avail much. It is my hope that this manual will offer you the tools you need to establish a vibrant, exciting prayer ministry in your church that will truly avail much!

PART ONE

◆

PRAYER ROOM BASICS

"We must not forsake the assembling of
ourselves together as priests who
communicate directly with God in prayer."
C. Peter Wagner

CHAPTER ONE

LOCAL CHURCH PRAYER ROOM

The purpose of the local church prayer room is to both promote prayer in the local church and to train laity to intercede for one another. One of the first decisions to make is whether or not your prayer room will have a phone line to receive prayer requests. In his book, *Making Room to Pray* (Prayer Point Press),[1] Terry Tekyl explains how to set up a prayer room without a phone line, with different stations for your intercessors. If you choose to set up a prayer room with a phone line, here are some guidelines:

1. The prayer line can be designated for use during certain hours of certain days, depending on your ability to monitor the phones. For example, you may be able to have someone available to answer the prayer line three hours per day on Monday through Friday, and one hour each Saturday.

2. Your prayer line should be an easy number to remember with the word PRAY at the end. For example: 464-PRAY.

3. Publicize your prayer line in the church bulletin and/or newsletter, including the hours and days the phone lines are open.

4. There are two kinds of intercessors in prayer rooms equipped with phones. They are "phone intercessors" and "silent intercessors." The primary function of the phone intercessor is to answer the phones and pray with callers, then log the prayer requests so that a PrayerGram (see Chapter 2) can be sent. Silent intercessor's prayer duties may include:

   a) Praying over phoned in prayer requests, either from cards or a computer print out.

   b) Praying over the prayer requests linked with the World Prayer Center in Colorado Springs. You can contact the World Prayer Center at:

      Rich Danzeisen
      World Prayer Center
      11005 Hwy. 83, #119
      Colorado Springs, CO 80921
      Phone: 719-262-9922, Fax: 719-262-9920
      Email: Rdanzeisen@wpccs.org

   c) Praying over church missionaries. (You may want to prepare a missionary notebook with bios, pictures, and prayer needs of your church or denominational missionaries for this purpose.)

   d) Praying for the church staff. (Again, staff notebooks with pictures of each staff member and their families may be helpful.)

   e) Praying over other notebooks of specific requests that may include a list of shut-ins, current prayer journeys, church concerns, or needs of church members.

      You can put the phone and the silent intercessors in the same room. If you do this, the silent intercessor can intercede for the phone intercessor while they are taking difficult calls. Another benefit of having them in the same room is that the camaraderie between the intercessors develops and they are able to share answered prayers. Another school of thought is to have separate rooms for the phone and silent intercessors. One benefit of separating them is that the silent intercessors can get more uninterrupted praying done. The second benefit is that the separation cuts out the temptation to talk and not to pray.

5. Decide how to answer calls that come in when phone intercessors are not available or are off duty. Voice mail or answering machines are an option, but silent intercessors should be trained to retrieve the calls before and after their prayer hour.

SECURITY OF THE PRAYER ROOM

Unfortunately, we live in a world where security is an issue— even in our churches and prayer rooms. For the safety of intercessors and prayer room staff, any church must think through and implement policies and procedures that help ensure security.

If the prayer room is open past church office hours, a combination locked door should be considered. Only the staff and assigned intercessors should be given the code. It is a good idea to change the code at least twice a year in case the word has leaked out. If you have 24 hour prayer, then a security guard is needed in addition to the combination locked door. For safety reasons, you may not want to encourage female intercessors to participate in the prayer room from 10:00 p.m. to 6:00 a.m.

LAYOUT OF THE PRAYER ROOM

1. The prayer room should be physically located near or adjacent to the prayer ministry office.
2. The prayer room should be in a strategic and accessible location near the parking area.
3. Believe God for nice furnishings including good desks, comfortable chairs, inspirational artwork, nice lamps, and so forth. This is a personal preference, but florescent lighting tends to be impersonal and harsh as opposed to soft lighting that provides an atmosphere more conducive to prayer.
4. The prayer room should have clean, fairly new carpet (many intercessors tend to spend a lot of time on the floor) and freshly painted walls in a soothing color.
5. Have a hallway/waiting area available for the intercessors to use as the shifts change.
6. Provide a restroom that is adjacent to the prayer room.

THE PRAYER ROOM "TO DO" LIST

1. Set prayer ministry staff in place
2. Recruit and train volunteers
3. Recruit and train intercessors
4. Report prayer needs to the church staff
5. Maintain sign-in sheets
6. Post prayer room guidelines (housekeeping, etc)

PRAYER ROOM PROCEDURES ATTENDANCE

1. Have the intercessors sign in upon arrival. This promotes promptness and accountability. Have new sign up sheets prepared the week before so the Monday morning inter-

cessors are ready to go.

2. If intercessors cannot come during their assigned hour, it is their responsibility to call another intercessor to cover for them. It should be stressed that they not leave their hour unattended for any reason! (You may want a prepared list of trained substitute intercessors available). For everyone's safety, and for the integrity of the prayer ministry, only trained and approved intercessors should be allowed in the prayer room.

3. Phone Intercessors: Stress that they are the only link between a church member and a minister during a time of crisis. Church members will call the prayer line in time of need, so they need to be ready to field the call properly.

4. Silent Intercessors: There is a tremendous need to pray over the calls and cards received each week. Continue to encourage the intercessors not to take this commitment lightly.

5. Have all intercessors take a moment each week to read current items on the bulletin board and the praise reports that are posted.

Phone Protocol

1. Devise a standard greeting for answering calls. One option is "God answers prayer! (Your church name), how may I pray with you?"

2. Listen carefully as the caller speaks and make notations on scratch paper. Obtain the necessary information to complete the prayer request card or type request into a computer program. Here is some information that should be included:

    a) A name is vital! If the caller is unwilling to give their full name, then get a first name.

    b) An address and phone number is needed for follow up.

    c) Hospital name, room number, and room telephone number.

    d) Church membership information is imperative because you will address the needs of members and their families first.

    e) Is the person for whom the intercessor is praying a Christian?

    f) Sign off with your name and daytime number (in case the prayer office needs clarification).

3. If the caller becomes repetitive or appears to want counseling, then summarize the prayer request and say, "Let's take this to the Lord in prayer." Do not ask the question, "Do you want to pray now?" Many will say "no" and continue to talk, in which case the phone intercessor has lost control of the call. Many times one or two people could dominate a prayer hour, so be sensitive to the Holy Spirit about how long to stay on one call. Stress to the phone intercessors that they are there to pray—*not* to counsel!

4. Ask the caller to call the prayer room with any updates concerning the prayer request and to call when the prayer has been answered.

5. **Always** pray at the end of each call. If the call is an update, pray again for that need. If the call is an answered prayer, offer praise and thanksgiving.

6. Use a caller I.D. system. All calls are to remain confidential. However, the caller I.D. system will alert the intercessor to problem callers. It can be utilized to obtain the telephone numbers of obscene or threatening callers. It also can be used to identify callers that are threatening suicide or reporting child abuse.

7. For reasons of security, a phone intercessor should **not** give his or her name to a caller. If asked they should simply reply, "I am an intercessor in the prayer room."

PRAYER REQUEST CARDS

The following is a suggested filing system for completed prayer request cards. While these suggestions refer to a physical card system, remember that a computer system of logging and listing prayer requests can also be adapted for the same purposes. The categories for this system are:

1. Today Box. This box contains a supply of blank cards and requests received within the past 24 hours.
2. Emergency Board. Urgent requests should be placed on the Emergency Board. Such requests would include:
   - Surgery—the hours preceding, during, and afterwards
   - A life-threatening illness or situation
   - Death in a family (until after the funeral)
   - Suicide
   - Child abuse, wife or husband abuse, runaway child
   - Other crisis situations
   The Emergency Board should not be a respecter of persons! Those requesting prayer do not need to be a church member to qualify.
3. Hospital Box. This box is for church members and/or their immediate family members who are hospitalized. The prayer office staff should maintain this box in order to keep the pastoral staff and the intercessors abreast of who is hospitalized.
4. Current Box. This box contains all the calls that the prayer room has received in the past few months that are not emergencies.
5. Anonymous Box. The cards in this box reflect prayer re-

quests submitted by a caller who wished to remain anonymous.

6. Long Term Prayer Need Box. These cards are considered serious needs that are too pressing to file in current boxes at this time. This box, along with the Anonymous Box, can be set on the Silent Intercessors' desk.

7. Frequent Caller Notebook. This book contains all of the frequent callers in alphabetical order. It is brought up to date monthly to keep it current. You may want to record the frequent caller's requests in this book rather than on a card in order to cut down on the number of cards, and so that a complete record of a frequent caller is kept. The names should be listed in the front of the book. A good plan is to look at that list when callers identify themselves or when their phone numbers appear on the caller ID system. Often lonely people or mentally challenged individuals will abuse the prayer line by calling each hour of the day all week long. The enemy can use this to block important prayer requests from getting through.

An important note: If a caller calls in with an update, and the intercessor can't readily find the card, just write up a new one. Never tell a caller, "I can't find your prayer request."

MINISTER ON CALL (M.O.C)

At least one of your ministers should always be "on call" for emergency situations involving members and their immediate families (spouse, children, stepchildren, parents, stepparents, siblings, grandparents, step-grandparents, grandchildren, or step-grandchildren).

The M.O.C. should only be contacted in cases of real emergency. Death of a church member or of the immediate family should always be considered urgent and demands that the M.O.C. be notified as soon as the prayer room receives the information. Other examples of emergencies include suicide threats, life-threatening illnesses or injuries, or emergency, unscheduled surgery. The pastoral ministry staff can generally handle routine or scheduled surgery on the next business day.

Make sure the caller gives complete information, including the phone number(s) where the concerned individuals can be reached. Then contact the pastor's office with the information. The prayer room should not contact an M.O.C. without a name and a telephone number where the caller can be reached. Unless your church policy differs, the M.O.C. should not be contacted unless the caller is a church member or a member of the immediate family.

CONFIDENTIALITY

All prayer requests should be considered confidential. Intercessors should be instructed not to discuss prayer requests with anyone once they leave the prayer room.

"Set a guard, O Lord, over my mouth; keep watch over the door of my lips" (Ps.141:3).

"I will guard my ways lest I sin with my tongue. I will restrain my mouth with a muzzle." (Ps.39:1).

SALVATION

When people call the prayer room with questions regarding salvation, intercessors should be familiarized with witnessing tracts or other tools to help guide the caller through a biblical plan of salvation.

Suicide Calls

If a caller states that he or she is thinking of ending their life, one option is to use the methods recommended in *The Billy Graham Christian Worker's Handbook* (Worldwide Publications).[2] Pages 227-230 of the *Handbook* show how to handle such calls, including the answers to likely questions and Scripture references for Christians and non-Christians alike.

Try to tactfully obtain the caller's name, telephone number, or any helpful identifying information. Otherwise, use the caller I.D. machine to obtain the information.

If the caller is a church member or a church member's immediate family member, and you have obtained their name and telephone number, call an M.O.C.

Obscene or Threatening Callers

Threatening or obscene calls are not only irritating and disgusting, they can be dangerous. The quickest and most effective way to deal with them is to remove whatever pleasure or satisfaction the caller is deriving.

1. As soon as an intercessor recognizes the nature of the call, hang up!
    a) Do not slam the phone down. When the caller realizes they have lost their audience they become discouraged.
    b) Do not preach to them or try to convert them. They may see this interaction as a competition and it encourages them.
2. More often than not, the caller will place another call right away. Note the caller ID and if it is the same caller, do not answer the phone. Let it go to the answering machine. If the ID device does not identify the caller, assume it is

he or she and let the call go to the answering machine.

3. If you do get them again on the line, follow the same procedure as above. Write a note to the intercessor that follows you to let them know what is happening.

4. After terminating such a call, alert the church Security Officer.

5. Write up a card with the details, Caller ID information, etc., and leave it for the Prayer Director.

6. "Call Block" can be instituted in most cases when the number is known.

7. Say a prayer for the offenders.

FREQUENT CALLERS

Make every effort to reduce or eliminate telephone calls from those who are abusing the system. By allowing them to go on and on repeatedly, intercessors are not helping compulsive callers, but are, in fact, enabling them. When compulsive callers fail to heed requests of limiting their calls to once a week, the Prayer Office may institute call blocking, preventing them from reaching the prayer room through that particular telephone. If they persist by calling from other telephones, the prayer room may turn the matter over to the church's Security office.

BENEVOLENCE

When a caller has a financial need and is requesting benevolence, instruct the intercessor to never make promises of money. Have your church policy available for the intercessors to share with callers asking for financial assistance. Have a resource manual ready so that the intercessor can refer them to benevolence agencies in your community.

Food/Drink

Most churches have a policy of no food or drink in the prayer room. Think this issue through and let the intercessors know what policy you have made. It is a good idea to post the policy in a highly visible place in the prayer room.

Personal Calls

You may also want to implement a policy regarding making or taking personal calls while on an intercessory watch. Many churches discourage personal calls as the intercessors are there to do a job and can easily become distracted by personal calls.

Notes

[1] *Making Room to Pray* is available through Prayer Point Press, 2100 N. Carrolton Drive, Muncie, IN 47304. Phone is toll free 1-888-656-6067 or 765-759-0215.

[2] *The Billy Graham Christian Worker's Handbook* is available through Worldwide Publication, 1303 Hennepin Avenue, Minneapolis, MN 55403. Phone is 612-333-0940

CHAPTER TWO

THE PRAYERGRAM
WRITER MINISTRY

The PrayerGram Writer Ministry is designed to send notes of encouragement to those who have requested prayer. Prayer requests can come from several places depending on the church's structure, including:

1. The phone line in the prayer room.
2. Calls received by the church staff.
3. Prayer requests written on pew cards and turned in during services.
4. Prayer requests from written pleas for help to the church.

Regardless of the source from which the prayer request comes, a note of encouragement can be sent.

DESIGNING THE PRAYERGRAM

The PrayerGram is an important tool for communicating the love of Christ in a time of need. They should, therefore, be nicely designed and printed. Here are some suggestions for

PrayerGram design:

1. PrayerGrams can be printed on postcards, fold over notes (which offer more privacy), or note cards with envelopes. Personal preference for taste, privacy, and cost determine what your prayer room will use.
2. Use the logo of the church or prayer ministry (if they have one) along with the address and phone number of the church and the prayer line phone number. Also, add the email address and web site, if applicable.
3. Put printed Scriptures on the PrayerGram, such as "Pray without ceasing" (1 Thess. 5:17), or "Stand in the gap..." (Ez. 22:30).
4. "Bright yellow paper stock is a must," says Donna D. Floyd from Tallwood Baptist in Houston, Texas, because the color stands out in the mail and represents the sun and the Son.
5. Leave plenty of space to write a personal note.

GUIDELINES FOR THE PRAYERGRAM WRITERS

1. Choose individuals who are not gossips and who will keep the prayer requests completely confidential.
2. Have the PrayerGram writers sign a waiver of confidentiality to impress upon them the seriousness of this commitment.
3. Train them to incorporate Scriptures into their notes of encouragement, because the Word of God brings life. Provide them a prayer promise book from which they can pull Scripture to use in their notes.
4. Ask them to pray over each request and be sure to ask the Lord which Scriptures to use.
5. Instruct them to be loving rather than judgmental, preachy, or critical.

6. Keep the notes to two paragraphs.
7. Have them sign their first name and the name of your church. Using first names provides a level of confidentiality. Each prayer ministry will have to decide its own policy and use it consistently.

LOGISTICS

If you have a heavy volume of prayer requests, assign one PrayerGram writer to each day of the week. For a lesser volume, have a few assigned for weekly duty. Try to not give each PrayerGram writer more than 20 notes per week, since you are encouraging them to pray as well. This can be time consuming.

Have folders with each PrayerGram writer's name on it for easy pickup of requests and drop off of written cards. The prayer office will stamp and mail these cards. Make sure clearly written names and complete addresses are provided to the PrayerGram writers. It is essential to choose people with legible handwriting, unless you are planning to use computers.

FRUIT OF THE PRAYERGRAM WRITER MINISTRY
FROM SUICIDE TO SALVATION

One day as I was working in my office, I received a knock at my door. A precious woman in her early twenties entered the room. She said, "You don't know me, but this ministry saved my life!" Her name was Barbara and she had called the 24-hour prayer line two weeks earlier. She had been seriously contemplating suicide. We were her last call. The intercessor on the 2:00 am shift that morning did an excellent job writing up the request.

The request was then passed on to a PrayerGram writer. A PrayerGram was sent within 2 days of the phone call. Barbara's comment to me was, "The words on that note gave me hope, and I have slept with it under my pillow for two weeks. Because of the love and encouragement showing me that God cared, I came to church here last week and gave my life to Christ." Barbara later became the lay leader of the PrayerGram writer ministry. She recruited, trained, and encouraged others with her powerful testimony of receiving a written touch.

CHAPTER THREE

THE GAP MINISTRY

So I sought for a man among them who would make a wall, and stand in the gap before Me on behalf of the land, that I should not destroy it; but I found no one. (Ezekiel 22:30)

PURPOSE

The purpose of The Gap Ministry is to bring intercessors together corporately in a designated location on the church campus to intercede for the church services while they are in progress. Intercessors pray specifically for:
1. The pastor, choir, all speakers, and soloists.
2. Those attending the service, especially the lost.
3. Baptismal candidates and their families.
4. For the Holy Spirit to touch lives through an outpouring of His anointing.
5. For the ministry time to be a blessing to those hurting and in need.

Logistics

When locating and equipping a room used for The Gap Ministry, there are several suggestions to take into consideration. The room should

1. Be accessible and easy to find.
2. Have a piano/keyboard or other instruments available so that worship is encouraged.
3. Have hymnals, Bibles, and songbooks available.
4. Have several copies of the order of service.
5. Have a large, blank notebook available for journaling revelation during the prayer time.
6. Be inviting with light, soothing colored walls, and spiritual artwork.
7. Have comfortable furnishings (not hard, cold folding chairs).
8. Have a bottle of anointing oil and boxes of tissue available.
9. Have prayer guidelines with Scripture references available.
10. Have a guide for each intercessor, explaining how to pray through the worship schedule.

Getting the Intercessors

Church members are encouraged to become Gap intercessors. They can participate by praying on a specific rotation (i.e., every two weeks, once a month, once a quarter, etc.). Most adult Sunday school classes, Bible study/prayer groups, or home groups will not mind being asked to participate in The Gap Ministry. Each group can be assigned a specific service for which they are to provide intercessors for The Gap Ministry. There is a real benefit to having groups who are accustomed to praying together and have developed a rhythm in prayer participate in this ministry. Deacons and their spouses, as well as youth groups, can also be assigned. Make sure you always have a minimum of two intercessors covering each service because the Bible tells us that there is power in the prayer of agreement.

STAFFING

The Gap Ministry is generally coordinated by one volunteer layperson. It will be that person's job to rotate the schedule and send out reminders in advance with a map of the Gap Room location. The coordinator follows up the letter with a phone call to ensure that each service in the upcoming week will be covered in prayer.

GUIDELINES

Think through what guidelines and/or rules you want to set in place and have these posted in the room in large print. For instance:

1. At the end of your assigned service, please make a journal entry of what the Lord showed the group or how you were led to pray.
2. Please do not eat or drink in The Gap Ministry prayer room.
3. Please leave the room tidy after your assigned service.

FRUIT OF THE GAP MINISTRY

As with any prayer ministry, there is certain fruit that can be expected from The Gap Ministry. They include:

1. Services that run more smoothly with less warfare.
2. More souls saved.

3. Greater anointing on the worship, the sermon, the offer-
    ing, the altar calls, etc.
4. Church members who enjoy an opportunity to take part by
    sowing into the services and witnessing the power of
    prayer.
5. A better understanding by the congregation of what effort
    goes into each church service.

———◆———

CHAPTER FOUR

THE WATCH OF THE LORD

I have posted watchmen on your walls, O Jerusalem; they will never be silent day or night. You who call on the Lord, give yourselves no rest, and give him no rest till he establishes Jerusalem and makes her the praise of the earth. (Isaiah 62:6-7)

PURPOSE

The purpose of the watch of the Lord is to build a wall of spiritual protection around the local church family by assigning intercessors to pray (usually off campus) in shifts covering all 24 hours in any given day.

LOGISTICS

There are many ways in which the local church could incorporate the watch of the Lord. Tom Hess's book, *The Watchmen*

(MorningStar Publications)[1] is the most thorough research available on this topic. Tom's ministry, called Jerusalem House of Prayer for All Nations, coordinates 24-hour prayer and praise watches globally. I strongly recommend that any church planning to implement the watch of the Lord utilize this tremendous tool made available by a seasoned practitioner.

One option for beginning this ministry is to recruit intercessors to pray one hour per week for the needs of the church family. They can pray from their homes, offices, or while travelling, which gives them the freedom to make a commitment to prayer that they might not otherwise make if they had to spend that time in a physical prayer room.

Prayer requests can be sent out in a monthly newsletter. Then as intercessors begin their prayer hour each week, they can call a "watchline" for current prayer updates. This way prayer for the most urgent and immediate needs of the church and the church family is being brought before the Lord continually.

The watchline should be an easy number to remember, for example: 222-PRAY. By calling, intercessors can listen to a prerecorded message that is updated weekly or as often as necessary in times of emergency. Make sure the watchline is set up so that intercessors can receive new prayer requests before they pray at their designated hour each week.

Another good idea is to have an intercessor just completing their watch call the intercessor just beginning the next watch in order to pass on information on how they felt the Lord leading them to pray. Benefits of this procedure include keeping continuity in prayer as well as increasing the level of accountability among the intercessors to their prayer commitment.

Recruiting and Maintenance

Assign a layleader to oversee this ministry. (You may or may not want to use military terms, for example, commander, captain, sergeant, etc.) That person would then assign a leader over each watch. The watch leader would be able to be in phone contact with everyone assigned to that watch. That way, in case of a church emergency, watch leaders could contact everyone in their watch.

Watches can be anywhere from one to three hours long depending on what is most feasible for your church. Half hour watches are not recommended because it can become too complicated to recruit enough leaders and intercessors to fill watch increments that small.

According to Mark 13:35, watches are three hour increments as follows:

6:00 a.m.-9:00 a.m.	6:00 p.m.-9:00 p.m.
9:00 a.m.-12:00 p.m.	9:00 p.m.-12:00 a.m.
12:00 p.m.-3:00 p.m.	12:00 a.m.-3:00 a.m.
3:00 p.m.-6:00 p.m.	3:00 a.m.-6:00 a.m.

Should you opt for three hour watches, Sunday school classes and cell groups can sign up for a watch and share the hours individually or corporately. The last watch, from 3:00 a.m.-6:00 a.m., is the hardest to fill. You may want to recruit shift workers, like nurses, who work night shifts and sleep during the day, because they are accustomed to these hours.

As you are setting up the watch of the Lord, you may find that you do not have enough intercessors to fill all the time slots. Therefore, you may want to fill only one or two watches per day or per week in the beginning. After intercessors have filled up those slots, then you can add additional watches. Before you know it, you could have around the clock prayer. Recruit shut-ins or people who are homebound from your church to help fill watches. These people often want to be useful, and prayer is something they can do effectively. Consider recruiting non-working people and retirees for the daytime hours. Usually, working people want the early morning slots before work and lunch hour slots.

Seek God for creative ways to recruit intercessors and keep them encouraged. Answered prayers are the blood that keeps the heart of the intercessor beating, so be sure they are kept up to date on how God has answered prayer. If all your intercessors have computers, you could set up an email system to send out weekly and monthly prayer requests. By linking together this way, intercessors could also email back to the prayer ministry with reports of how the Lord has lead them in prayer during their watch. Another added benefit of being computerized is the ability to connect with the World Prayer Center for international prayer requests in addition to local church prayer needs.

Maintenance is the key to keeping this ministry up and running. Make sure the newsletters are mailed out on time so they are received by the last day of the month. This way the 6:00a.m. intercessor of the first day of the new month has the up-to-date prayer requests. The same principle applies to keeping the watchline recording updated.

THE SYSTEM

1. Individuals participating in the watch of the Lord commit to give one hour each week to intercessory prayer for:
   a) their families

b) the church family
c) other requests as listed in the monthly newsletter or on the watchline.
2. Monthly newsletters will provide:
   a) prayer thoughts
   b) prayer promises
   c) a list of church activities to be supported with prayer
   d) missionary needs
   e) prayer requests on current issues
   f) answers to prayer
3. Watch of the Lord Intercessors may pray wherever they are – at home, the office, or on vacation.
4. Commitment and responsibility to pray at the appointed hour is between the intercessor and God.
5. Watch of the Lord intercessors will also be asked to pray when telephoned with prayer alerts that are initiated by the pastor and are of church-wide importance.

FRUIT

The watch of the Lord is an effective way to mobilize an entire church of any size to pray. Not only will it get your people involved in the prayer ministry, but it also has the potential to increase both the quantity and quality of prayer in your church.

Notes
[1] *The Watchmen* is available through Jerusalem House of Prayer by calling toll free 1-800-542-0278. Otherwise, please contact MorningStar Publications 16000 Lancaster Highway, Charlotte, NC 28277.

PART TWO

---◆---

BEYOND CHURCH WALLS

"Through prayer you can touch the life of
anybody, anywhere, regardless of their
circumstances or distance."
Dr. Charles Stanley

Through prayer, the body of Christ has a unique opportunity
to reach into the community and make a real difference. There
are many creative and effective ways to structure prayer that
is intended to minister the love of Christ to individuals who
may never receive prayer otherwise. This section outlines
five prayer programs to help you get started in taking prayer
beyond the walls of your church and into a community des-
perately in need of a touch from God.

—————◆—————

CHAPTER FIVE

Shield a Badge with Prayer

The purpose of Shield a Badge with Prayer is to provide daily prayer (and thus, a shield of prayer protection) for local police officers, fire fighters, and their families.

Logistics

1. Assign a layleader to coordinate this ministry who is competent on computers. Also recruit volunteers who are willing to do data entry and maintenance.
2. Recruit intercessors that are willing to make a one year commitment to pray for an officer/firefighter and their families every day.
3. Meet with city or county police and fire stations. The first order of business is to set up an interview/fact finding meeting with the department heads who can make the decisions.
4. Make it clear that you are offering a confidential prayer

partner from your church with absolutely no strings attached, who has committed to pray daily for one year for the safety of an officer/firefighter and their family.

5. Have the officers/firefighters who want to participate fill out a card that explains the ministry, objectives, and details (see example on pages 42-43). If the officers/firefighters choose to do so, they can list their spouse's and children's names to be prayed for as well.

6. Log the various police and fire stations along with the police officers and firefighters on computer. Match the intercessors with their officer/firefighter. Some intercessors may want more than one officer/firefighter. You may also have some couples, families, Sunday school classes, or cell groups that commit to praying for an officer/firefighter. This is a great idea, but be sure to assign only one contact person.

7. Inform the assigned intercessor who their officer/firefighter is by supplying the name, badge number, and station address.

8. As soon as intercessors receive their officer/firefighter, you may ask them to write a letter of introduction and encouragement within the week. If the officer/firefighter desires to write back that is their decision. No expectations of ongoing communications should be expected.

9. This ministry is not to be used for proselytizing, although prayer for salvation is greatly encouraged.

Fruit of the Shield a Badge with Prayer Ministry

1. This ministry provides greater physical protection for those who watch over your county, city, and region.

2. Intercessors can pray for the salvation of unsaved offic-

SHILED A BADGE WITH PRAYER 41

ers/firefighters in addition to providing a spiritual covering that the officer/firefighter may not otherwise have.

3. You can expect to see a drop in the divorce rate of officers/firefighters because of this added spiritual protection. Their marriages are challenged with higher levels of danger, pressure, and fear than the average marriage.

4. This ministry can expand to other churches in the community. You may recruit intercessors from as many denominations as you have officers/firefighters. For example, Baptist police officers might be matched with a Baptist intercessor and so forth. This kind of interchurch effort can help bring unity in a city as you see prayer bring down denominational walls.

5. This ministry can help transform a community.

SHIELD A BADGE

WITH PRAYER

CHURCH NAME & ADDRESS

A ministry to protect our law enforcement with prayer

In these troubled times, the role of a police officer is becoming more difficult. The men and women who serve as "the thin blue line" are not only facing a physically more perilous task, but also one that is emotionally and morally draining.

The Shield A Badge prayer ministry has been successful in other parts of our nation. The goal of this ministry is to involve all interested residents of the local area in a commitment to pray daily for safety, good judgment, and a safe return home each day for law enforcement officers in our area. Shield A Badge is an opportunity to demonstrate our support and concern for the officers and their families. If you would like to make a sincere commitment to pray for an officer on a daily basis for one year, please complete the form on the other side.

Officer _____

Badge Number/Rank _____

Agency/City _____

Office Address _____

City _____ St _____ Zip _____

Church Name _____

Please return this card to the Prayer Ministry Office
(Include Address and Phone of your church)

Prayer Partner _____

Address _____

City _____ St _____ Zip _____

Phone (H) _____ (W) _____

Church Name _____

Would you like to pray for more than one officer?

How many? _____

Guidelines:

1. This is a commitment for one year by the prayer partner (citizen) to pray daily for the safety and wellbeing of an assigned officer and his or her family.

2. Only the officer's name, badge number, and agency will be given to the prayer partner.

3. Communications from the prayer partner to the officer are to be limited to holiday greeting and no more than four pieces of mail per year. The correspondence will be sent to the agency that employs the officer.

4. No effort is to be made by the prayer partner to make personal contact with the officer. Cards and notes to the officer via his agency will be sufficient.

5. The prayer partner is encouraged not to send gifts of any kind to the officer.

6. If the officer leaves his or her agency, the prayer partner will be notified and another officer will be assigned. If for some reason the prayer partner cannot fulfill the commitment, he should notify the Prayer Ministry Office.

7. The prayer partner should enter into his ministry with no ulterior motives. No expectations whatsoever are placed on the officer. The prayer partner is to expect nothing from the officer or the agency in return for prayers he renders.

8. The prayer partner may, if he wishes, use his name and address on correspondence to the officer, thereby allowing the officer to respond, if he or she desires to do so.

—————◆—————

CHAPTER SIX

CRADLE A CHILD
WITH PRAYER

It is true—Jesus loves the little children! Luke 18:16 says, "Let the little children come unto me." The purpose of Cradle a Child is to provide prayer cover for little children, their families, as well as the daycare centers. This may be the only time in a tender young life that some of these children have ever been prayed for.

LOGISTICS

1. Use the same methods of recruiting and assigning intercessors as were used in Shield a Badge. Parents should fill out cards.
2. Some churches have day care programs. If so, you can start by matching intercessors with children in your own programs. If not, choose a day care center in your community.
3. The same principles of confidentiality that applied to

Shield a Badge apply to Cradle a Child. The notes of encouragement are sent to the day care center.

4. Again, no phone contact or personal meetings are encouraged unless the parents of the child initiate it.
5. Make sure the lay leader of Cradle a Child develops a good rapport with the day care administrator.
6. Remember, this ministry is not to be used for proselytizing, although prayer for salvation is encouraged.

FRUIT

1. Little ones will be protected through prayer spiritually, emotionally, and physically.
2. Parents and siblings will also benefit from this prayer cover.
3. This ministry allows you to be a part of seeing lives changed and healed.
4. Day care centers are spiritually held to higher integrity levels.
5. This ministry can help transform a community.

CHAPTER SEVEN

ADOPT A LEADER

Therefore I exhort first of all that supplications, prayers, intercessions, and giving of thanks be made for all men, for kings and all who are in authority (1 Tim. 2:1-2).

The purpose of Adopt a Leader is to assign intercessors to pray for city officials and their families.

LOGISTICS

1. The first decision to be made is which city/county leaders to target in intercession. The number of intercessors and the size of the community will be the determining factor.
2. The intercessors will need to be given a prayer guide of Scriptures showing how to pray for those in authority. This prayer guide should also include the names and positions of those in office on the state and national level as well. These names include the U.S. President and cabinet, your state's governor and cabinet, and your state's representa-

tives and senators.

To help with developing a prayer guide, Susan Sorensen has written an excellent daily prayer calendar on praying for those in authority called Adopt-A-Leader Daily Prayer Calendar. You can order the calendar by contacting: Michigan Family Forum, P.O. Box 15216, Lansing, MI 48901-5216. Their phone number is 517-374-1171.

3. Like all of the prayer ministries that have been mentioned, this ministry will need to be computerized and updated as leadership changes.
4. Adopt a Leader intercessors can also gather corporately during election seasons to pray for voter turnout and godly appointments.

FRUIT

1. This ministry promotes awareness in the church body of the importance of Christians taking responsibility about electing leadership in our country.
2. Government leaders may become more open to making godly decisions as the Holy Spirit moves on them through prayer.
3. This ministry can draw new groups of intercessors into the overall prayer ministry. For example, men are often more interested in praying for leaders than they are in other prayer ministries.

CHAPTER EIGHT

PrayCare
for the Elderly

The purpose of this ministry is to intercede for those in assisted living programs and their immediate caregivers.

Logistics

1. Recruit intercessors from your church and/or extend this ministry to other churches in your community.
2. Use all the same principles of recruitment, assignment, and confidentiality as Shield a Badge and Cradle a Child.
3. Start with your church members and their families who have relatives in assisted living programs.
4. Move on to one retirement home and meet with the administrator.
5. Because those in assisted living programs are often lonely, notes of encouragement should be written more often, perhaps on a bimonthly basis.
6. Sunday school classes, cell groups, etc., may want to adopt

a "grandparent" to be a part of the PrayCare ministry.

FRUIT

1. Prayer for the elderly is so rewarding because the elderly can be the loneliest people around.
2. Prayers of salvation are particularly important because most of these individuals are at the end of their lives.
3. This ministry is a witness and a comfort to immediate family and/or the caregivers.
4. This ministry is a real witness of the love of Christ to the entire retirement facility and their personnel.

CHAPTER NINE

MEDIPRAYER

This ministry is to intercede for medical professionals (doctors and nurses) who work in emergency rooms and are faced with trauma and death on a daily basis.

Logistics

1. Seek out medical professionals in your local church and/or your Christian circles and ask them which emergency rooms might have an interest in this ministry.
2. Use all the same principles of recruitment, assignment, and confidentiality as were outlined in Chapter 5.
3. With this specific prayer ministry, connections are best made through existing personal relationships.

FRUIT

1. Prayers for emotional stability and endurance can lessen

the burnout, health, and marital problems that result from the intensity of this profession.

2. This ministry could be a real encouragement to the medical profession in a hospital or small emergency clinics.

3. Bringing Christianity into a world that handles life and death is always an asset.

PART THREE

---◆---

MAINTAINING AN EFFECTIVE PRAYER MINISTRY

"A church cannot afford a boring prayer ministry any more than it can afford a boring worship service."

Terry Teykl

CHAPTER TEN

PRAYER MINISTRY TRAINING

NEW INTERCESSOR ORIENTATION/TRAINING

To train and equip the phone and silent intercessors assigned to the prayer room, a weekly or bimonthly orientation should be advertised in the church newsletter and Sunday bulletins. Information that should be included in orientation sessions was outlined in Chapter 1.

SCHOOLS OF PRAYER

Spring and Fall Schools of Prayer can be used to recruit new intercessors for the prayer ministry and deepen the understanding of prayer. If you have more than one component of the prayer ministry, it is good to bring them all together. Also, invite the whole congregation to the Spring and Fall Schools of Prayer. It is a personal choice depending on several variables, but consider doing one or both schools at an encampment outside of town. When you get people into a quiet setting away from distractions, it helps them to focus more clearly on the Lord.

Bring in a speaker/teacher for the School of Prayer that can really impart and stir a hunger in the intercessors for prayer. Have an allotted time for testimonies to encourage the intercessors and build their faith by hearing the answered prayers.

NOTE: Reports of answered prayers are the lifeline of an active, motivated prayer ministry.

Be sure to make personal and corporate times of prayer a priority. Choose an anointed worship leader to lead each session into the presence of the Lord. Have the lay leader from each area of the prayer ministry to teach a workshop with sign-up sheets available for new recruits.

You will want to create an exciting atmosphere at these Schools of Prayer. After all, what could be more awesome than talking with the living God. Have warm, outgoing, friendly people to be greeters and registrars at the retreat. It makes for a good start. Make the sure the promotion of the retreat is done with months of notice and publicity. Assign a committee to handle each aspect of the retreat, such as the making of the nametags, preparing prayer journals and packets for each individual, etc.

Ask the pastor to dedicate a Sunday or Wednesday service to teaching on prayer. Perhaps your church could even have a designated month of prayer. Always provide prayer ministry sign-up materials at each gathering.

LEADERSHIP RETREATS

Annual prayer ministry **leadership retreats** should be done off campus to provide a time of refreshing, refocusing, equipping, strategizing, and evaluating needed changes. All prayer ministry staff and lay volunteer leaders should be included.

CHAPTER ELEVEN

PRAYER MINISTRY APPRECIATION

The purpose of prayer ministry appreciation is so that the volunteers that are not being paid, yet have committed to giving hours of their time, will feel appreciated for a job well done. Any encouragement goes a long way and helps keep morale boosted. Here are a few options for showing those involved in the prayer ministry how valuable they are and how grateful the church is for their service:

BANQUETS AND LUNCHEONS

A. Annual intercessors/volunteer prayer banquet
   1. Send out invitations a month in advance.
   2. Get a great speaker.
   3. Give recognition awards for achievements such as best attendance, most number of hours volunteered, and so forth.
   4. Give small gifts of recognition to bless your interces-

sors and volunteers that will remind them of the prayer ministry, such as mugs with the church or prayer ministry logo on them.

B. Volunteer appreciation luncheon for those who help with computer entry, paper work, phone calls, and all other important volunteer work that keep the prayer ministry running smoothly.

  1. These luncheons can be scheduled around the holidays or during summer lulls.
  2. Luncheons can be held at the church, in homes or at a restaurant. If done at a restaurant, the prayer ministry needs to pick up the tab.
  3. It is a nice touch to have a little something to give them, like an embossed Bible promise book.
  4. Encourage them with answered prayers and praise reports from the prayer ministry.
  5. Create an atmosphere to make them feel special and appreciated.

OTHER FORMS OF APPRECIATION

A. During the month of prayer (see next chapter), list lay leadership and/or volunteer names in the church bulletin with a note of thanks.

B. Notes of thanks go a long way. Because the Christmas season may be too busy to send personalized notes, you might consider sending personalized Thanksgiving or Easter cards.

CHAPTER TWELVE

PRAYER MINISTRY PROMOTION

Prayer ministry promotion is the key to growing and maintaining an effective prayer ministry.

INTERNAL PROMOTION
(WITHIN THE PRAYER MINISTRY)

A. Monthly Newsletter
   1. List upcoming events in the prayer ministry.
   2. Post openings of available prayer hours in the prayer room and with the Watch of the Lord.
   3. Include articles of exhortation or excerpts of prayer from well known prayer leaders.
   4. Include a recommended reading list of key books on prayer that cover a wide spectrum of prayer topics.
   5. List answered prayers that are not confidential and can be shared.
   6. Itemize prayer ministry needs such as volunteers, in-

tercessors, leadership, PrayerGram writers, etc.

B. Incentive programs to help recruit new intercessors. The goal is to get the entire congregation to participate in the prayer ministry in one area or another. Here are some suggestions for suitable incentives:

   1. If someone signs up one new intercessor for any prayer ministry, they receive a beautiful prayer ministry mug.

   2. If someone signs up two new intercessors they receive a leather bound prayer promise book with their name and the church's name engraved on the front.

   3. If they sign up five or more intercessors, they automatically receive a scholarship to the upcoming (fall or spring) prayer retreat.

EXTERNAL PROMOTION
(TO THE WHOLE CHURCH)

A. Use prayer request pew cards

   1. Design these so they are small enough to fit in a pew slot or as an insert in the church bulletin.

   2. Create plenty of room on the pew card to write out a detailed prayer request.

   3. Design the pew card so that there is a place to indicate interest in becoming an intercessor in the prayer ministry.

   4. Make sure the pew card requests the name and address of the person filling out the card so that a PrayerGram can be sent.

   5. The pew cards should end up in the prayer room to be prayed over after being reviewed by the prayer ministry staff.

   6. These pew cards are an excellent non-threatening way to identify the needs and hurts of the local body.

7. Pew cards could be a way to launch a church prayer ministry by providing prayer requests to the prayer room.

B. Have weekly prayer announcements in the church bulletin. You may want to include church needs, names of those hospitalized, names of those whose family has suffered a death, and the name of a pastor to be prayed for throughout the week.

C. Place regular announcements/articles in the church newsletter.

D. If your church has TV monitors, advertise prayer events/ training on these monitors and keep them up to date.

E. Write a brochure to promote the prayer ministry that includes each aspect of the prayer ministry. Be sure to include scheduled weekly training sessions, annual prayer events, and a response section that can be filled out and returned to the prayer office. This brochure can be placed around the church or included it in a mailing to the congregation.

F. Choose one month each year as a designated month of prayer.

1. Make it consistent from year to year by using the same month. For example, May would be an excellent month because the National Day of Prayer is always the first Thursday in May.

2. Include creative prayer reminders in the weekly bulletin and/or church newsletter.

3. Include a prepared prayer event each week.

4. You may want to schedule a School of Prayer during this month.

5. Another option for your church could be doing a "Solemn Assembly" during the month of prayer. I recommend the *World Intercession Network* materials by Bane and Barbara James, PO Box 12609,

Oklahoma City, OK 73157, Tel: 405-787-7110, Fax: 405-789-3957. This Solemn Assembly could be just for your local church or could be opened as a citywide event that would require a lot more preparation and planning.

G. In the United States, participate in the National Day of Prayer on the first Thursday of every May.

1. Make sure your prayer ministry is registered to receive National Day of Prayer literature and information from the national office. The National Day of Prayer office provides a packet of prayer guides, prayer bookmarks, and other tools helpful in praying for America. You can order these items by calling 1-800-444-8828.

2. Have the church chapel/sanctuary open for several hours, such as from 6:00 a.m.to10:00 p.m. on that day. Encourage all the prayer ministry intercessors, church members, and others who want to participate to come by and pray for the nation during those hours.

3. Have a sign-up sheet available to record the names, phone numbers, and addresses of all who come to intercede. You can then follow up and see if they want to be part of the prayer ministry if they are not already involved. Place your prayer ministry brochures on the sign-up table to inform people of the prayer ministry opportunities and how to get involved.

4. Get the youth of the church involved in the National Day of Prayer. One way is to pray around the flagpoles at their schools, which is referred to as "See You at The Pole." Think of creative ways to interest youth in prayer. The National Day of Prayer is an excellent introduction to prayer for youth.

5. You can go beyond your church family and open your church facility to your community. To do this you

might want to:

- Have an evening praise and worship/prayer service during the National Day of Prayer. If you do, it is important to soak the service in prayer. You may also want the worship team to be composed of musicians from several different churches.
- Run radio spots on Christian stations to get the word out.
- Invite all churches involved in Shield a Badge, Cradle a Child, or other prayer ministry areas and be sure to invite all the officers/firefighters for whom your church prays.
- Be sure to coordinate with other churches in your community for any city wide events.
- Have an intercessory team with a designated prayer leader assigned to cover this prayer ministry event before, during and after the National Day of Prayer
- Above all, remember to be inclusive and rally prayer!

H. Hold church-wide monthly celebration services. The purpose of these praise/prayer services is to provide an opportunity for corporate praise watches which often produce prayer focuses, or a corporate sense of how to pray in the coming month. One of the benefits of these celebration services is that your people will learn to enter into corporate worship, which will encourage more personal worship.

1. Create a time slot for a mini devotional or short teaching, but keep the speaking to a minimum with a focus on praise and worship.
2. Worship teams can be rotated so that this is not a burden on your church worship leader. These services can bring forth and help promote new talent/hidden

giftings. Consider using youth bands.

3. Have prayer ministry brochures available which provide an opportunity to recruit new intercessors.

I. Periodically conduct an all-night prayer meeting.

1. Invite everyone, especially prayer ministry intercessors involved in the Prayer Room or Watch of the Lord ministry.

2. Have snack breaks and aerobic breaks to stay awake.

3. Have at least two worship teams lined up.

4. Try to use a room with carpet and comfortable chairs.

INSTITUTE PUBLICATIONS

RIDDING YOUR HOME OF SPIRITUAL DARKNESS
Chuck D. Pierce
& Rebecca Wagner Sytsema

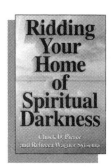

Christians are often completely unaware of how the enemy has gained access to their homes through what they own. This practical, easy-to-read book can be used by any Christian to pray through their home and property in order to close the door to the enemy and experience richer spiritual life. Included are chapters on children, sin, generational curses, and spiritual discernment, as well as a step-by-step guide to praying through your home and a section of questions and answers.
Paperback (75 pp.) • 0.9667481.7.4 • **$7.20 (save 10%)**

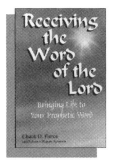

RECEIVING THE WORD OF THE LORD
Chuck D. Pierce
& Rebecca Wagner Sytsema

The Bible makes it very clear that God has a plan for our lives. By hearing and receiving the voice of God, we can know our purpose and destiny. In this book you will discover how to hear the voice of God, develop an understanding of prophecy, learn how to test a prophetic word, and experience the joy of responding to God's voice.
Paperback (41 pp.) • 0.9667481.2.3 • **$5.40 (save 10%)**

HOW TO CAST OUT DEMONS: A BEGINNER'S GUIDE

Doris M. Wagner

Many modern Christians are now agreeing that we should take Jesus' command to cast out demons more seriously than we have. But how do we do it? Where do we start? This practical, down-to-earth book, written by a respected deliverance practitioner, will show you how.

This one-of-a-kind book will help you to:

- ♦ Take authority over demonic spirits
- ♦ Conduct a private 2-hour prayer appointment
- ♦ Administer a 15-page diagnostic questionnaire
- ♦ Break bondages of rejection, addiction, lust, and more
- ♦ Bring inner healing and break soul ties
- ♦ Set free those whom the enemy has held captive

All this rooted in solid, biblical integrity and done in a calm, safe, controlled ministry environment.

Paperback (201 pp.) • 1.58502.002.8 • **$10.80 (save 10%)**

From C. Peter Wagner . . .

RADICAL HOLINESS FOR RADICAL LIVING
C. Peter Wagner

Can anyone really live a holy life? Is there a test of holiness? *Radical Holiness for Radical Living* answers these and other questions as it opens the way for you to move to new levels in your Christian life. You can defeat Satan's schemes and enjoy daily victory in your walk with God.
Paperback (41 pp.) · 0.9667481.1.5 · **$5.40 (save 10%)**

HARD-CORE IDOLATRY: FACING THE FACTS
C. Peter Wagner

This hard-hitting book is destined to clear away the foggy thinking about idolatry that has permeated churches today. This book will help you recognize idolatry (even in some of our churches), confront the schemes of the enemy with more understanding and power, feel the pain of God's broken heart when His people worship idols, and begin to cleanse your home of idolatrous objects.
Paperback (43 pp.) · 0.9667481.4.X · **$5.40 (save 10%)**

REVIVAL! IT CAN TRANSFORM YOUR CITY
C. Peter Wagner

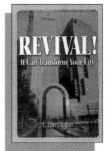

This book answers many questions including: What exactly is revival? Can my city actually be transformed through revival? What steps can be taken to sustain revival in a city? Discover how the Spirit of God can visibly transform our cities through the revival for which we have been praying!
Paperback (63 pp.) · 0.9667481.8.2 · **$5.40 (save 10%)**

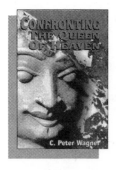

Confronting the Queen of Heaven

C. Peter Wagner

This book takes a look at what is perhaps one of the most powerful spirits in Satan's hierarchy--the Queen of Heaven. This book answers what we as Christians can do to play a part in confronting the Queen of Heaven and proclaiming that Jesus Christ is Lord.

Paperback (42 pp.) • 0.9667481.3.1 • **$5.40 (save 10%)**

Praying Through Turkey
An Intercessor's Guide to an Ancient and Needy Land
Andrew Jackson
with George Otis, Jr.

This book will take you on a fantastic journey, tracing Christianity from its roots to modern times in the nation of Turkey. Intercessors will receive invaluable instruction on how to pray for the cities and unreached peoples of Turkey.

Paperback (60 pp.) • 1.58502.000.1 • **$5.40 (save 10%)**

Coming soon from Wagner Institute Publishing:

◆ The Authority of the Believer and Healing
   by Dr. Che Ahn

◆ Supernatural Architecture
   by Dr. Stan DeKoven

◆ Pulling Down Strongholds
   by Hector Torres

◆ The Strategic Prayer Room
   by Chuck D. Pierce & Rebecca Wagner Sytsema

For credit card orders please:
call *toll free* 1-888-563-5150
or fax 1-719-266-8256
or email: Arsenal@cpwagner.net

Or mail order with payment to:
The Arsenal
P.O. Box 62958
Colorado Springs, CO 80962-2958 USA

For bulk orders please:
call: 1-719-277-6776
or email: Wlsales@cpwagner.net

All international orders must be paid by credit card

Name

Street Address
(Cannot deliver to P.O. Box)

Phone

Title	Product Number	Qty.	Total
	Subtotal (carry this amount to other side)		

Order form continued . . .

Shipping Rate Table for US only		Subtotal (from other side)	
Amt. of Subtotal	Add		
$50 and under	$5		
$50.01-$60.00	$6	CO residents add 6.01% sales tax	
$60.01-$80.00	$8		
$80.01-$100.00	$10		
Over $100.00	10% of order		
For international orders, please call or fax with credit card. Shipping will be calculated for you.		Shipping (see table)	
		Donation to GHM	
		TOTAL ENCLOSED (US FUNDS ONLY)	

Please allow 10 days for delivery. International orders may require
6 weeks for delivery.

METHOD OF PAYMENT:

☐ Check/Money Order (made payable to The Arsenal)
☐ Credit Card: ☐ [VISA]   ☐ [MasterCard]   ☐ [Discover]

Number: _____

Exp. Date: _____ Signature: _____